let us play I SPY camping!

i spy play books by
© Little Dezign Press

ready to play
i spy camping?

just like real i spy game, letters are
not in alphabetical order.

i spy with my little
eye, something beginning with...

f

f is for...

fish!

i spy with my little
eye, something beginning with...

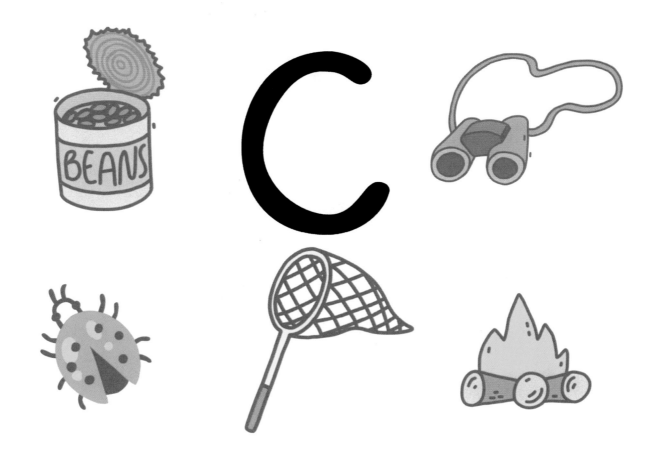

C

C is for...

campfire!

i spy with my little
eye, something beginning with...

l is for...

lantern!

i spy with my little
eye, something beginning with...

m

M is for...
matches!

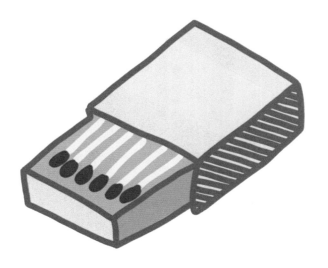

i spy with my little
eye, something beginning with...

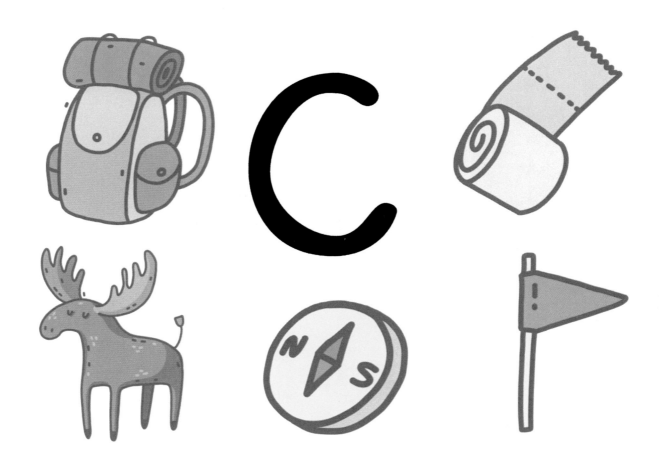

C is for...
compass!

i spy with my little
eye, something beginning with...

b is for...

bear!

i spy with my little
eye, something beginning with...

a is for...

axe!

i spy with my little
eye, something beginning with...

t is for...

tent!

i spy with my little
eye, something beginning with...

n is for...

net!

i spy with my little
eye, something beginning with...

K is for...

kite!

i spy with my little eye, something beginning with...

g

g is for...
guitar!

i spy with my little
eye, something beginning with...

S

S is for...

snake!

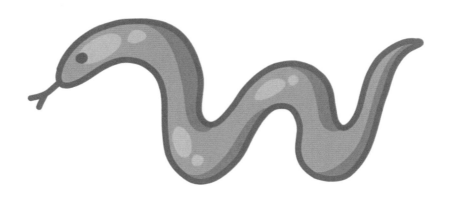

i spy with my little eye, something beginning with...

h is for...

hat!

i spy with my little eye, something beginning with...

M is for...

mushroom!

i spy with my little
eye, something beginning with...

C

C is for...

camera!

i spy with my little
eye, something beginning with...

r

r is for...

radio!

i spy with my little eye, something beginning with...

S is for...

shovel!

i spy with my little
eye, something beginning with...

M is for...
map!

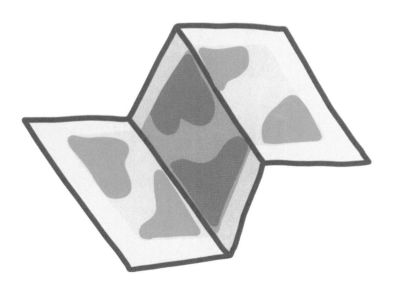

i spy with my little eye, something beginning with...

b is for...

backpack!

Made in the USA
Middletown, DE
19 September 2020